Everyday expressions

Kyiah Evans

Presentation by *BookLeaf Publishing*

Web: www.bookleafpub.com

E-mail: info@bookleafpub.com

ISBN: 9789357748391

First edition 2023

*To the people who taught me strength,
passion, and love. Without you, I would not
be who I am today.*

ACKNOWLEDGEMENT

Thank you to everyone who made this book possible, from those who sat and listened to me edit and re-edit as I would try my best to share my work, to those who have allowed me the opportunity to write this collection in the first place.

PREFACE

The story of life is a wonderous one, every moment carries the smallest of crumbs that, if you look carefully enough, hold what it means to be alive. This is just a short collection of a few moments that have been captured in time. I hope these stories reach those who need them, and perhaps along the way can help someone who maybe feels a little bit like me, feel a little less alone.

Purple Lace

Within the glass along the beach I walked in the
fading light,
A castle stood upon the sea with rays of gold
and gray.
The setting sun was falling fast and with it left
the day,
But above the spires of the king left a crown of
purple lace,
And within the jewel is where I live above the
beauty's face.
The melting glass against the sun began to wash
away,
Within my hand the kingdom stood until the end
of day.

Tomorrow's joy

They say that it gets better,
that time will heal all wounds,
they say that it won't last forever,
but every night I'm in my room,
the cold, dark, heartache comes creeping back
inside.

I hear your voice a whisper,
as fleeting as the wind,
I feel your touch caress me,
my pale and frozen skin.

I remember the way it sounded when we'd laugh
till the morning light,
I remember the way it felt to hold you close to
me at night.

They told me it wouldn't last forever,
that the pain would soon subside,
that soon your smile would be a memory that I
could recall with joy in time.

I remember the sinking feeling,
the nausea,
and the pain,

what it felt like to try to breathe every time I
heard your name.

And so it goes, life moved on and I soon caught
up too.
My world had changed,
and I had too,
But some things never do.

Surrender

The light purples and yellows cast onto the silent
pews.
All souls have since long abandoned the
testimonial palace.
The old wood creaks under the weight of the
mice,
The only inhabitants that remain.
I sit on the dark oak, warped by the years of
burdened sinners,
Looking up into the light spilling through the
stained-glass of the chapel windows.
Golden rays warm me to my core.
A withered dusty cross hangs behind the
podium,
Once a testament to strength.
I'm reminded of the blood spilt,
The communion shared here with disciples.
The scarlet drops like the melted wax rolling
down the edge of midnight candles,
The torturous cries of a man,
A child,
Begging for an answer.
"Why God! Why have you forsaken me?"
The silence that answers is deafening.
The dark droplets will dry,

But the word will always remain.
A child,
A victim,
A tortured soul,
Trapped within a world scripted by the roll of
dice that hold the cold exhale of death.
A scarred word is all that remains of that night
tested by fate,
Victim,
The scarlet lettering now pale,
Jagged letters carved into the ivory skin.

Creature with your name

I have stared into this oblivion, fallen
Victim to its pull. Memorized its
Depths, but I am one of the rare ones, I survived.
For the oblivion is not an
Empty void. Blackness hides its heart, and there
lies a
Beast. A creature that purrs
Your name, calling out, hypnotizing you unto the
Infinite depth that so many
Crave to understand. Then as you
Float into its center the beast strikes. Ripping
from the
Darkness itself. Metallic claws drenched in the
blood of
Past souls. Green scales covering its body. Its
teeth
Flash before you with a smile so sweet,
Dripping with poison honey. The cold, dead
Stare finally has its source. It searches your
Soul, before it begins to pull at the
Threads binding you together. The creature
engulfs
Your body. Wrapping itself around you like a
Snake going for the kill. Your breath

Hitches as your lungs scream for air. You tense and
Begin to fight. A soft hum begins to
Reverberate from the creature's throat, lulling you to
Sleep. Your heart stops, your
Blood no longer flowing. A calm
Peace overtakes you, with a flash the creature's teeth
Sink into your flesh.

Every Day's Masterpiece

Someone told me today that when you can tell
your story and not cry, you know you have
healed.
But that's not really true.
I have gone through my story and told and retold
the tale,
But I have never truly healed.
Even now I look like I may know what is to
come,
But I still stumble and think to myself,
"My god, what if they figure out, I have no idea
what comes next?"

Midnights prayer

May the moon sink low
and the darkness fade.
May the sun rise
and the sky shine blue.
May the air be warm
and the breeze blow soft.
Let my mind calm,
As I bask in the day that comes.

Untitled

The sun
and the moon
and the stars themselves
marveled at her,
For she was exactly
who she always wanted to be.

Iridescent Waters

I've seen it,
The end.
I have lived through the horrors,
The violent, reckless, needless deaths,
I have felt the pain and loss,
The regret of, "Did I do enough?"
I am a child,
I know not of these things
And still,
I have lived them.
Again and again
we make the same mistakes,
wishing,
praying,
pleading for another outcome.
And yet,
the fury of the cosmos continues to rage on;
Ebbing and flowing
far past our mere existence.
Time is a river that flows,
constellations,
schools of fish that shine
in the iridescent water.
The current itself
the passionate fire that burns through.

Pushing along,
Dragging the unsuspecting souls
like sand,
unsettled from its slumber
on its ocean floor.

Their stage

My mind races,
My pulse quickens,
All I can see in front of me is an empty stage,
On which I am expected to perform.

A masterpiece is held before me,
A torch passed down
to a girl who
once upon a time… slayed a beast.

I once had magic that flowed through my veins,
I stood tall and faced the dark.
Though it was a minor battle in most eyes,
the war that raged on out of sight was merciless.

Now, again,
I am expected to perform.
Show the world what I have become,
the hero that they all have come to expect.

I am no hero.
I am still just as lost as I was when my journey
began.

To be

To be loved is to know what it is to be the beauty of the stars in the heavens.
To be wanted is to be given the power to create the stars themselves.

She knows better

She knows not to fall, not to listen to the empty
promises and bittersweet lies.
She is the one who sees the monsters in the dark
and knows what they will do.
She has fallen before, seen the hunger in their
eyes as they claw at her skin and sink into her
flesh.
She has kicked, screamed, and fought to stay
above water and in the end, she won.
Yes,
She is the one who knows better because she has
lived in the dark,
She has preyed on the ones who once were like
her, lost and blind to see the wolf lurking nearby.
She is the one who knows better, who has tasted
the innocent blood,
She hid in the dark fighting a war that she now
fights from the other side.
She is the one who knows better, she left her
world behind
To find a place she knew existed, somewhere
within her mind.
She kicked, screamed, and fought and in the end,
she won.
Yes,

She is the one who knows better,
She cares for the ones who fall prey to the dark
and warns those others away.
She smiles so brightly you'd think her naive,
But you see,
She is the one who knows better
And she is the one who kicked, screamed, and
fought and in the end, she won.
But when the dark again falls and the monsters
appear she still falls into their hands,
Believing the empty promises and bittersweet
lies.
In the hopes that she can see the light in their
eyes.
For she is the one who knows better,
Better than to believe the stories told.
She knows it will hurt, that her heart will shatter.
She knows how the pain will swallow her whole,
And she knows,
That in the end,
She will still fall,
Because she is the one who knows better.

Youth

A gift squandered,
Drapes shroud the fragility of life,
Lights twinkle as the snow falls
Blanketing the oblivion.
Blush red lips tender kiss,
Hot bodies clinging to sheets,
Heavy breaths break through silent thoughts of
Pain
Pleasure
Ecstasy and
Regret.

The unwanted

They danced until dawn in the fire lights glow,
at home in their skin for everyone to know.
They called themselves deviants, traitors, and freaks,
for these were the names that no one did seek.
At home with the wolves,
The howling beasts.
At home with the trees,
Where they shared in their feasts.
They shared in the joy of their chaos and mess,
They shared in the joy of their peace and their rest.
They screamed and they cried and they ran with bare feet,
For these were the ones that would not be beat.
The embers burned down and the fire did fade
But when came the dawn, they stood unafraid.
For they were the wild ones at home in unrest,
For they were the warriors with blood on their chests.
I stand before you as one of them now,
For I seek my peace and lay my old life down.

Am I Enough?

Listen to my next words, tomorrow
I will be gone and nothing
Save the wonders of mystery
Will remain. I had
Hoped that within this
Black dash that encompasses
Every heartbeat, every
Breath that I may come to
Find what it is they call
Love, the one thing we
Die for,
Fight for,
Burn from the very center of my
Core for. Listen to my words that
Speak true. breathing life into a
World vacuuming my soul from my
Lungs. The dark
Embraces as arid
Poison replaces life, you will
Fight for your place upon broken
Steps to a marble
Palace. The fear rising
Within your chest as you
Hesitantly stumble to your
Judgment.

The Greatest Adventure

Pay attention Ana,
For when you arrive at the port
You must see the man in the uniform.
He is the only one who will be
able to help.
By the time you return
I must be gone.
Off on an adventure of riches
And danger.
My work will remain and you,
You must slave through the
Hot coals that burn the backs
Of men too cowardice to go
On their merry way.
Let the breeze dry your sheets
On the line outside of your
Stone-built house.
Let the rains nourish the growing
Sapling before it is cut down
And used to burn.
Let the earth give you all the
Splendor and love that I have,
And when we meet again you
Will give to the earth all of
You that remains, and
Join me in paradise.

A World Renewed

Beating down on the roof
A cacophony of white noise

Suffocating all life

I remember my grandmother
Drying my soaked clothes
As I warmed my hands in the hot sink water.
The smell of hot chocolate milk
Overpowers my senses.
My dark wet hair in ringlets
Clinging to my small body.
The power had gone out, but the rain
Battered down.

The world calms
An eerie still washes over
My heart chills.

Hope,
Have hope is what I'm told
For this will all be over soon.

I hear the screech of rubber, the

Sparks assault my eyes like fireworks seen from the
Docks on the fourth of July.
Metal grinds,
My eyes fill with tears.
I beg
"Please."
"Please."
Air is ripped from my lungs
My body tensed
My world goes dark.

Raindrops wet my face
Thunder rumbles above my head
The world is renewed
And I am at its mercy.

For Myself

Precious is life to he who holds dear,
a thought of what life could be like without you
here.
I know of a woman who sits by the river
I see her standing like stone against the world
she now faces alone.
She had a son, the light of so many,
He would bring her flowers and remind her that
life is worth living.
No one could know of the demons he hid,
His smile was so bright
and he was just a kid.
I know of a young girl who cries every night
Tears stain her cheeks and her eyes grow heavy
with sleep.
She was just a child in her pink little room
when the world began to ask too much of her all
too soon.
Now she pierces and tattoos all that she can
and tries to forget the feel of her skin,
and still, no one sees what is lying within.
I know of a man who works day and night
His face caked with sweat and his hands
calloused and bloody.
He busies himself with work, cars, and beer

And aches for a day he doesn't feel so alone,
Then he is reminded that this is not home.
There is a light of hope and strength,
A fire that burns within everyone,
Life is a gift for everyone else,
And life is a gift that I fight for myself.

Existential life

Beloved mountain wonder, manifesting serenity,
peace,
to narrate the adventure, the journey of truth.
Time lacing radiance,
the crimson oceans bewilderment in the tyranny
of genesis.
To create hope is to derive disdain and malicious
song from the siren Riverbend.
The aristocratic monarch, now serendipitous to
the scarlet survivor.
Divided generosity, the desire for home.
A reflection of elegance,
of majesty,
of the philosophical,
of life.

Radiance

A Flower,
Forever encased in glass,
Years after it has been plucked from the vine.
Though withered and fragile,
Still holds the same beauty it once did.
The stars danced in the sky.
Music spun around us as the world blurred.
His strong hands firm on my hips,
My own draped around his neck.
It's in these moments of timelessness that we all
share.
Our deepest, most intimate hearts,
That pull at the strings of every life.
His breath was shaky,
Mine stead-fast.
Those precious seconds,
Before.
My heart pounds.
And then,
Like fireworks bursting from the seams,
A hot passion erupts.
That flower was new then,
Its beauty, radiant.
Its fragile petals now wilt.
Pain has marred what now remains.

Yet still,
Its elegance endures,
Growing in strength,
With each new year,
With each new break,
In its delicate surface.

Your Memory

An old white stove stands at the far wall, its top
stained yellow with years of frying up meals,
the burners no longer work in places and the
heavy black cast iron skillet still sits on the right
side.
If I close my eyes now, I can still see it…
The warm spring sun cascades through the high
windows,
The oil pops and sizzles in the pan,
The smell of fried chicken wafts through the air.
I am home for a moment wrapped in your arms,
Flour covered and laughing.

Where the Water Flows

The afternoon shines brilliantly through the
evergreen boughs of the pine tops,
Speckled glory land on my skin,
its warmth has been gone for so long, winter
days filled with frigid frozen ground,
now the water springs to life rushing down the
stream flowing along the banks of the shore,
heated by the sun.
I sit alone and listen to the birds sing,
Winter is gone, I reach the edge of the cliff,
Almost noon now I close my eyes and listen to
the pounding of my heart,
This is who I am, this is where I belong.
This is where the water flows.

www.ingramcontent.com/pod-product-compliance
Lightning Source LLC
LaVergne TN
LVHW010914200726

843509LV00013B/1935